FACING
THE APOCALYPSE

Also by Bud Harris, PhD

Sacred Selfishness: A Guide to Living a Life of Substance

Aging Strong: The Extraordinary Gift of a Longer Life

The Journey into Wholeness: A Jungian Guide to Discovering the Meaning of Your Life's Path

Becoming Whole: A Jungian Guide to Individuation

The Midnight Hour: A Jungian Perspective on America's Current Pivotal Moment

Confronting Evil: A Jungian Guide to Searching for Light in the Heart of Darkness

Radical Hope and the Healing Power of Illness: A Jungian Guide to Exploring the Body, Mind, Spirit Connection to Healing

The Search for Self and the Search for God: Three Jungian Lectures and Seminars to Guide the Way

Cracking Open: A Memoir of Struggling, Passages, and Transformation

The Father Quest: Rediscovering an Elemental Force

Resurrecting the Unicorn: Masculinity in the 21st Century

The Fire and the Rose: The Wedding of Spirituality and Sexuality

Students under Siege: The Real Reasons Behind America's Ongoing Mass Shootings and How to Stop Them

Co-authored with Massimilla Harris, PhD

Into the Heart of the Feminine: Facing the Death Mother Archetype to Reclaim Love, Strength, and Vitality

Like Gold Through Fire: Understanding the Transforming Power of Suffering

The Art of Love: The Craft of Relationships: A Practical Guide for Creating the Loving Relationships We Want

FACING
THE APOCALYPSE

---◆---

A Call for Outrageous Courage, Love, and Compassion

Bud Harris, PhD

DAPHNE PUBLICATIONS, AN IMPRINT OF SPES, INC.

Harris, Clifton T. Bud
Facing the apocalypse: a call for outrageous courage, love, and compassion / Bud Harris.

ISBN: 978-0-578-32395-4   Nonfiction
1. Jungian psychology 2. Personal growth

Cover and Layout Design: Courtney Tiberio

CONTENTS

"Any real change implies the breakup of the world as one has always known it, the loss of all that gave one an identity, the end of safety. And at such a moment, unable to see and not daring to imagine what the future will now bring forth, one clings to what one knew . . . or dreamed that one possessed. Yet, it is only when a man is able, without bitterness or self-pity, to surrender a dream he has long cherished or a privilege he has long possessed that he is set free—he has set himself free—for higher dreams, for greater privileges."

—*James Baldwin*

Foreword

Over a decade ago I opened a lecture I was giving by recounting a dream I had during a crisis period in my early forties. In the dream I found myself sitting in the front of what was then called a Shoney's Big Boy restaurant. The booth I sat in was next to the large front windows. While I sipped my morning coffee, I looked out onto the main street of the town I grew up in.

As I turned my head and looked across the table, I saw a small boy with rumpled brown hair and intense blue-gray eyes. Shocked, I realized he was a five-year-old version of myself, before tragedy struck our family. When I looked into his eyes, he quietly said, "What have you done with my life?"

Before I could answer, I awakened. As I was musing over the dream, I knew that the boy hadn't been talking about the surface stuff like going to the office, shopping, dieting, or even making a living for my family. Those sensitive eyes were searching for a more serious answer. That small boy, Buddy, was posing the question to me that life asks of us all. And that question is not, "What is the meaning of my life?" It is, "What meaning am I creating with my life?" That question is still alive in me today.

My answer is to try to fully engage in life, so that I can develop a greater awareness of my reality and the truth of my existence, so that my life will have an evolving purpose, values, and a way of being fulfilled. And I am seeking connection with life's spiritual aspects and the spiritual depths within myself, so that I can be sure that love is the foundation of how I live.

Now, if you asked me how I am pursuing this complicated-sounding task, I would answer by telling you that I am doing my level best to live Dr. Carl Jung's individuation process. Jung's individuation process is one of our greatest gifts from the twentieth century. The process facilitates the conscious and intentional healing of ourselves and developing of the potentials in our unique personality. A brilliant healer of the body and soul, Jung brought us a new way to use the imagination and the experiences of creativity and love.

It was the ideas in Jung's individuation process that challenged me to become more fully engaged in my life and life in general. Jung was strongly convinced that only a full engagement in life can give us the necessary material for reflections that can transform our consciousness. In individuation, reflecting upon a life being lived is meant to teach us more about ourselves, to increase our daily self-awareness, to expand our consciousness, and to guide us in cultivating our capacities to love. Without mincing words, Jung told a convention of pastors in 1932 that we must be willing to take risks and make mistakes and that, if we are fully engaged in life, we will be in a position to learn from and even be transformed by our failures.

Shortly after this dream, I made a 180-degree turn in my life and began the journey to becoming a practicing Jungian analyst. I also began to write.

Ever since, writing has helped me bring order out of chaos. It helps me focus on understanding my experiences, my life, what is happening to me and around me. The threatening chaos we have been experiencing—from the toxic political atmosphere of the 2016 presidential election, the emboldening of White supremacists, the climate crisis, and the COVID-19 pandemic—have roused my emotions. As part of this writing project, I wanted to understand why. This awareness is crucial because my emotions tell me when my boundaries have been violated, as well as when my life has been turned upside down. Emotions reveal my most profound values, and ultimately, no matter how rational I believe I am, they are the power behind my decisions. It is important to include them in this writing process because they make my life real, and the process encompasses a great deal more than simply seeking solutions. In addition, the emotions I have failed to face and integrate all too often become the driving force behind my temperament, health, and decision making, which results in their detriment.

These emotions also keep reminding me of Buddy's question, "What have you done with my life?" I wonder what he might think of how I've answered his question. In the chaos of today's world, I wonder even more. While I am wondering, I remember a story told by Auschwitz survivor and Nobel Laureate Elie Wiesel:

A just man decided he must save humanity. So, he chose a city, the most sinful of all cities. Let's say it is Sodom. So, he studied. He learned all the art of moving people, changing minds, changing hearts. He came to a man and woman and said, "Don't forget that murder is not good, it is wrong." In the beginning, people gathered around him. It was so strange, somewhat like a circus. They gathered and they listened. He went on and on and on. Days passed. Weeks passed. They stopped listening. After many years, a child stopped him and said, "What are you doing? Don't you see nobody is listening? Then why do you continue shouting and shouting? Why?" And the man answered the child, "I'll tell you why. In the beginning, I was convinced that if I were to shout loud enough, they would change. Now I know they won't change. But if I shout even louder, it's because I don't want them to change me."

This story moves me deeply. It isn't why I work or why I write, but in the midst of today's chaotic world, it reminds me how strongly I must hang on to the values of the heart and of the soul. It reminds me to be a seeker.

I know that I need to find meaning in my shock, my sorrow, my anger, and even in my fatigue.

I have encountered more sorrow than I could have imagined at the number of people dying, and at how they are dying. I have lost people in my community, and people in my practice, some of whom worked with victims of the pandemic. And I've lost members of my family. I've talked by cell phone with people so ill they wanted to die, with families who have suffered suicides, with healthcare workers who are too broken by the pain they are witnessing to return to work. I know people are dying terrible deaths, alone, no one close to comfort them, to touch them, to speak to them, to pray with them or over them. I have witnessed loved ones and families who cannot see the dying to comfort them or even remember their face for a last time. There is more and it brings inconceivable grief.

I have encountered shock like I could never have imagined—shock that people I was taught to respect will do almost anything, say almost anything, and ignore almost anything to gain and hold on to power. I am just as shocked at how much support these people can get. I am shocked at how the pandemic has revealed the failure of our national character to show that we care about one another. I am shocked that the most powerful and richest nation in history is so driven and manipulated by fear.

I have encountered anger like I have never experienced or imagined. I am enraged that we have given rise to politicians and media sources that seem to behave like genetic mutations that awaken and cultivate anger, fear, rage, despair, and cowardice in people until they become threatening social illnesses, making our whole society sick. Political and media figures make huge amounts of money and gain significant power exploiting people's deepest fears, resentments, desperations, and hopes.

I know most of us are tired of the pandemic. We are tired of being afraid, isolated, lonely, self-disciplined, worried about our finances, unable to see the future, and unsure of how to deal with schooling and all the other challenges the pandemic has brought. But it is important to remember that we were in a crisis, an apocalypse, before the pandemic. An apocalypse in a psychological sense is an unveiling of a severe reality that has been previously present but unseen. It is what we refer to in Jungian psychology as an archetypal pattern in human nature. The pandemic has intensified this apocalypse and revealed aspects of it that, for many of us, had been hidden, but the pandemic did not create it.

With that in mind, facing our sorrow brings us deeper into our humanity. It can open our hearts even if it breaks them in the process. Of course, it seems rational to want to return to some kind of normal or to envision a new normal, leaving this pandemic behind us. But as many of us know deep within ourselves, these longings aren't possible and can only be an illusion, a temporary escape from the true reality we need to face.

If we truly accept our sorrow, and even our shock and anger, they can become the impetus for a new journey. Similar shocks motivated Prince Siddhārtha—once he encountered the realities of poverty, illness, and death—to begin the journey of becoming the Buddha. Suffering in a Nazi death camp compelled Holocaust survivor Dr. Viktor Frankl to seek to understand the vital necessity of humanity's search for meaning, and to share it with the world. The true realization of suffering will compel us into action beyond our self-interest. Frankl, Jung, and a history of great souls have revealed to us that beneath our search for easy answers and happy endings, we are more profound creatures who seek meaning, purpose, self-transcendence, and love as the foundations for living. I work and write in the hope I can contribute to this process.

PART I

—⋅◆⋅—

Unveiling Reality

"*I have often seen patients simply outgrow a problem that had destroyed others. This "outgrowing," as I formerly called it, proved on further investigation to be a new level of consciousness. . . . The insoluble problem . . . was not solved logically . . . but faded out when confronted with a new and stronger life urge. . . . I had learned that all the greatest and most important problems of life are fundamentally insoluble. . . . They can never be solved, but only outgrown. I therefore asked myself whether this outgrowing, this possibility of further psychic development, was not the normal thing, and whether getting stuck in a conflict was pathological.*"

—Carl Jung

INTRODUCTION

❝ Where love stops, power begins, and violence, and terror" (*Collected Works* [CW], vol. 10, par. 580). This quotation from Jung, which is central to my discussion, has haunted me for over four decades. In the face of this statement, I feel the need for myself, our society, and even our world to live with courage, love, and compassion, the intensity of which is bold, unusual, and startling. We must find within ourselves a level of courage, love, and compassion that awakens us and calls us into action that is, in fact, outrageous. Another of Jung's observations is crucially important to our society and our world situation today. Jung writes that "the individual's feeling of weakness, indeed of nonexistence, was thus compensated by the eruption of hitherto unknown desires for power" (CW, vol. 10, par. 454). As you will see, these statements describe conditions that can pave the road to an apocalypse.

In the first statement Jung is talking about two of our most profound human instincts: love and power. When a major instinct is wounded, it creates a psychological complex that is compensatory to it. When our love instinct is damaged, our power instinct increases its weight and strength. It works very much like a traditional scale with plates suspended at equal distances on either side. When a psychological complex comes into play, it works like a weight that makes one plate descend while the other plate rises in a compensatory manner. So, when our love instinct is wounded, we begin to develop a power complex. The heavier the wound, the stronger the compensation will be. A major complex that results from a damaged instinct forms a complete emotional system that can take over our personality when it is triggered, even becoming a dominant force in our personality if the wound to love is sufficient. When left unconscious—that is, not recognized, faced, and healed—such a complex becomes dangerous. It will seek goals. It will seek goals beneath our everyday awareness that, though we will attempt to justify them rationally, are secretly directed by our fear, weaknesses, inadequacies, and early wounds to love. Our goals will be pressed into the service of our dominant complexes. This circumstance is as true for us collectively as it is personally. When left unconscious and unhealed, a power complex will initiate severe conflicts. When made conscious and healed, which is no small task, the capacities of both of these instinctual forces can work together to enhance our lives in numerous ways. As I will explain in the latter part of this book, a fulfilling life needs both love and power in balance.

Examining the first quotation, "Where love stops, power begins, and violence, and terror," we can immediately see a reflection of our society, which means "we" as a whole. We have lost our footing and gone too far to the power side. No one can deny the serious factional disputes breaking out in our country and around the world, and the horror accompanying them shows what our political scene has become. There is a general disintegration of the societal and moral values that have long been the structure of our society. These values are no longer defined and supported by our religious institutions or the democratic ideals that our nation has traditionally aspired to. These tendencies have become so widespread that they are causing waves of public infection that spread even to people who previously had enough psychological and spiritual strength to resist them. These conflicts—and the chaos, confusion, and destructiveness they are causing—are accurately symbolized in the apocalyptic mythologies in our histories. Unfortunately, the chaos is distracting us from fully facing and dramatically acting to change the destructive course we have set for our planet.

We human beings have been given a terrible gift: we are able to make choices and, to varying extents, be the authors of our own stories, which will then make up our collective stories. The chaos in the world bears witness to the wrongness of many of our choices. We have made too many choices out of willful naivete or ignorance because we didn't want to face the challenges of making truly informed choices. Such choices can be made only when we possess profound self-knowledge and a thorough understanding of human nature and history. We know from the myth of Oedipus that when he was at a crossroads, he killed a man he didn't know and wasn't aware this man was his father. Then he married a woman he did not know and wasn't aware she was his mother. Tragedy followed. Jung explains to us that "before the bar of nature and fate, unconsciousness is never accepted as an excuse; on the contrary there are very severe penalties for it" (Joseph Campbell, ed., *The Portable Jung*, p. 637).

It is in this spirit, to help us know and understand ourselves better, that I am sharing my reflections on, my explanations of the current state of the archetype of the apocalypse in our country, its psychological meaning, and the way each one of us needs to respond to it.

—·+·—

Thoughts and Questions to Ponder...

Upon finishing this first intense section, find a quiet, comfortable, safe place and take a few moments to settle into yourself.

Take some deep breaths and let your mind wander back over what you have read. Now let me invite you to spend some time writing on the pages we have provided, or in your journal, about what you experienced while you were reading. What were some of the ideas and feelings that came up in you?

As you continue, you might consider these questions: When you think of Jung's statement, "Where love stops, power begins, and violence, and terror," what do you think he means? Where in your own experiences have you seen this statement playing out?

Were you surprised by his assertion that "the individual's feeling of weakness, indeed of non-existence, was thus compensated by the eruption of hitherto unknown desires for power"? Have there been times in your life when you felt diminished and devalued, perhaps early in your life or even later? Do you better understand how the realities of these two statements can affect our worldview and goals in life?

As you reflect upon this section, can you think about, and record in your journal, what it means to you to recognize that both love and power are basic human instincts that need to be recognized and cultivated through self-awareness?

Consider the idea that we are given a terrible gift in the ability to make choices. It is often humbling to see how easily we make them without knowing how to truly think them through. How might aware-ness of these realities challenge you to further examine how you are living?

Other Thoughts?

———•✦•———

THE ROLE OF AN APOCALYPSE

An apocalypse occurs when a realization or an event causes the abrupt end or destruction of one's own world or of an entire civilization. An apocalypse is also an unveiling of a reality, or a potential reality, that has been there all the time but that we had not seen clearly before. It is also an unveiling of our own lives' darkness, which we have avoided acknowledging. In addition, an apocalypse makes it clear that there is no "normal" we can return to. We must recreate ourselves based on a new psycho-spiritual value structure and a new openness to the future. If we have the courage to look into the causes of the apocalypse and the meaning of the darkness it unveils, we will begin to see a path for change. In our case looking into the darkness reveals that we live in one world and that we try to isolate ourselves at our own peril. This process also reveals our wounds to love, to our capacity to genuinely care about ourselves and one another; in trying to compensate for this wound and its resulting fear and vulnerability, we have pursued power. The latter part of this book is devoted to healing this wound to our love instinct. In the case of a person, a wound to this instinct fractures, and often destroys, the structure of psychological, moral, and spiritual values that support the person's identity and the direction and meaning of their life. All too often a person has allowed their society's values to determine a large part of their identity structure. So, a personal and a societal apocalypse are clearly related. A society can suffer an apocalypse in the same manner as a person can. This is because a society also has a collective identity structure. You might say it has an "ego," which is the conscious attitudes and values that run the show of the everyday life of the society. A society also has a "persona," a public face that pictures the attitudes and behaviors it deems acceptable and appropriate and that further the goals of the society. Society likewise has a "shadow," or dark side, where the attitudes and behaviors that it doesn't deem acceptable are repressed beneath its appearance. Of course, that is all oversimplified, but I will expand on the topic later.

As a person, I also have a Self, with a capital S, which Jung defines as a greater entity that contains our ego and our personal and collective unconscious. The Self includes a pattern or storyline that represents the potential one's life is meant to express. It also includes the "life force," which acts as the creator and carrier of all our preexisting, built-in patterns of behavior. The Self is the cause of our individuation process, the drive to become a complete and fully developed person. Because individuation involves creation and recreation as a growth process, individuation is a life's work. This psychological structure is complicated to understand, but it is necessary in order to help us make choices. Individuation involves joining our conscious intelligence, the ego, with the greater intelligence of the Self and with the instincts of the unconscious. Then we are no longer identified solely with our ego or with our instinctual, unconscious impulses and complexes without being aware of them.

Because we have a Self that has a developmental direction and we combine to make up our society, we can also say our society has a developmental force that determines its trajectory. When a society becomes too one-sided, too unbalanced, when it loses its psycho-spiritual grounding, the archetype of the apocalypse may be activated to devastate the destructive direction of the society, causing it to start over again in order to recreate its "civilization." For example, as I remember the Old Testament, in many cases when the children of Israel strayed too far away from God, they were conquered by another people and taken into captivity or visited by plagues, famines, and other forces of an apocalypse. In psychological terms, instead of using the word *God*, we would say this was the challenging intervention of the Self calling for a profound transformation of psychological and spiritual values and structures and a creative generation of new ones.

Thus, we would have a new vision for the purpose and meaning of our lives or that of the society.

— ⋅∤⋅ —

Thoughts and Questions to Ponder...

As you sit back and reflect on this section, ask your-self how you have thought of an apocalypse in the past. Did you think of it as some kind of esoteric religious imagination? Did you think of it simply as fate? Does this reading help you understand that an apocalypse is a happening and an experience we must seek to understand?

Write in your journal what comes to mind when you consider that an apocalypse occurs when an event or a realization turns one's world upside down and unveils a "reality, or a potential reality, that has been there all the time but that we had not seen clearly before."

What are some of your reflections on how our per-sonal identities and value structures intertwine with our society's social character and values? Does it make sense to you that a society can suffer an apocalypse in the same way a person can?

How surprised or shocked are you by the dark side of our society that is being unveiled? How much have you tried to avoid seeing this dark side clear-ly and seeking to understand it? Have you thought about why you have not seen it sooner?

Other Thoughts?

A PERSONAL EXPERIENCE
OF AN APOCALYPSE

In our personal lives we can encounter a number of apocalyptic kinds of experiences. I would like to share the story of one that inspired me and that gives us some good advice for facing our societal apocalyptic experiences. When I first encountered author Reynolds Price in the 1990s, he was delivering a presentation at Malaprop's bookstore in Asheville, North Carolina. He was full of gentle humor and vitality. He made the presentation on his newly published book in an easygoing way from his wheelchair. Almost a decade before, at the peak of his career as a writer and a professor at Duke University, doctors discovered a large cancer on his spinal cord. He then went through over four years of multiple radical surgeries and severe radiation treatments that left him paralyzed. He writes about that journey in words almost too direct to bear when reading his book *A Whole New Life*. He uses the term "catastrophic" to describe it. Catastrophic comes from the Greek word, *catastrophe*, which means "an overturning or upending." It is very close to meaning "an apocalypse."

Let us look at some of his advice, because it is full of very helpful, practical intelligence:

"Grieve for a decent limited time over whatever parts of your old self you know you'll miss."

"Have one hard cry, if the tears will come. Then stanch the grief by whatever legal means."

"Next find your way to be somebody else, the next viable you—a stripped down whole other clear-eyed person, realistic as a sawed-off shotgun, and thankful for air."

"The kindest thing anyone could have done for me, once I'd finished five weeks of radiation, would have been to look me square in the eye and say this clearly. 'Reynolds Price is dead. Who will you be now? Who can you be and how can you get there double-time?'"

"What are the thoughts and acts required to turn your dead self inside-out into something new and durably practical that, however strange, is the creature demanded by whatever hard facts confront you now?"

It is obvious, I believe, that it took **outrageous courage** for Reynolds Price to face the words, "Reynolds Price is dead. Who will you be now?" Also, it took **outrageous compassion** for him to move beyond the physical pain and face the psychological, emotional, and spiritual pain, all of which he had never even imagined as a possibility. And then it took **outrageous love** for him to act, to choose once again to commit to an entirely new and creative approach to living. He also describes the attitude we should have to our new life:

"Meanwhile whether you see yourself as the temporary home of a deathless soul or as the short-term compound of skin and bone called *Homo sapiens*, your known orders are simply to *Live*. Never give death a serious hearing till its ripeness forces your final attention and dignified nod. It will of course take you screaming if it must, if you insist."

No advice can inspire or move me more than the insistence on "choosing life" from someone who, like Reynolds Price, had to make that choice. In my experience, all too often we end up miserable at the end of our lives because we have failed to choose life, individuation when we had the chance.

———•✦•———

Now, I wonder, what if we were to apply Price's advice to the apocalyptic situation in our country right now? What if we said to ourselves that the old America, however we may have conceived of it, is dead? To start our consideration of this question, we will look at what an apocalypse really means and what it reveals about ourselves. And we will try to do so in a way that is "clear-eyed" and as "realistic as a sawed-off shotgun."

A new life, a transformed life, for Reynolds Price included dealing with paraplegia and choosing life rather than despair, though not without intense suffering. His personal apocalypse and his ability to face it head-on left him a hard-nosed realist, yet a more compassionate, patient, watchful, and inspired writer and teacher.

———— •∤• ————

Thoughts and Questions to Ponder

Price's story, I believe, deserves our deep reflection. We can view it as a representation of life's journey. It reminds me of the writings of Spanish theologian Miguel de Unamuno. In his book *The Tragic Sense of Life in Men and Nations*, he gives us the blessing, "May God give you no peace but glory!" Price's story gives life to this blessing, as he had the courage to face reality and the love of life to fulfill its potential by creating a new self and a new life.

Does this story help you understand that even in the face of great loss, if we acknowledge and face it as a reality, there is a new potential future?

What was your response to the statement, "The kindest thing anyone could have done for me, once I'd finished five weeks of radiation, would have been to look me square in the eye and say this clearly. 'Reynolds Price is dead. Who will you be now? Who can you be and how can you get there double-time?'"

And how did this question affect you, "What are the thoughts and acts required to turn your dead self inside-out into something new and durably

practical that, however strange, is the creature demanded by whatever hard facts confront you now?"

Since our individual identities come together to
make up the identity of our society, whether it is
unified or fragmented, can you imagine applying
Price's advice to our national apocalypse today?

Other Thoughts?

———•✦•———

PART II

---·❖·---

Facing the Heart of Darkness

"*Knowing your own darkness is the best method for dealing with the darknesses of other people. One does not become enlightened by imagining figures of light, but by making the darkness conscious. The most terrifying thing is to accept oneself completely. Your visions will become clear only when you can look into your own heart. Who looks outside, dreams; who looks inside, awakes.*"

—*Carl Jung*

FACING REALITY

Over the years I have realized that as much as failures may brutalize my self-esteem, my greatest transformations began with failure. I have also learned to overcome some of my fear of encountering these events. Sometimes I even desire them. Through these experiences, I have learned that we are defined by what troubles us, not what reassures us. I recognized long ago that I have never been transformed or learned anything significant from success. So, I generally look at failure as the first step on a new journey. We often need to start some part of our lives all over again. Moreover, as I have emphasized, we need to face these moments of change head-on, with a courage supported by a love of life and energized by an inner quest for self-awareness and growing consciousness.

Self-awareness and growing consciousness are crucial because, no matter what we think, we all live in a self-inflicted condition of limited awareness of reality. Hindu philosophy calls this condition *maya*, or a state of illusion. For us to be truly aware of our reality, we have to know a great deal about our shadows and the dominant psychological complexes that shape our worldview. Let us look at an explanation that, although greatly oversimplified, describes how this state of illusion can come about.

If we don't get the love, safety, and affirmation we need in the first eighteen months of our life, we will internalize the feeling that the world is a hostile place and we won't be capable of feeling secure in it (severe traumas while growing up may have a similar effect). These experiences generally become a dominant complex. This complex governs how we see the world and puts us into an adversarial relationship with it. We may find ourselves facing conflicts with a fight, freeze, or flight response. We will have an irrational distrust of other people and institutions. We will often be vulnerable to social, political, and religious manipulations that play on our fears. When we feel weak or diminished, we may find that explosions of anger give us a sense of power and standing in the world. We are afraid of feeling vulnerable or weak and of not having our right to exist validated. Anger becomes our protective shield.

If we don't become aware of our dominant complexes, we will always be susceptible to outside manipulation on many levels. Good advice is often to "face reality and deal with it." But if we haven't recognized and worked through our dominant complexes, what we think is reality is usually far from it. This brief explanation illustrates that self-awareness and facing the truth of our lives are crucial for living a meaningful and fulfilling life. The very same is true for our social character and the advancement of our culture.

Becoming aware of our personal complexes and shadows—while difficult and often shocking, constituting our own little apocalypse—will help us realize potentials we haven't known, and that transformation always means a change of heart. We will be faced with the task of creating a new structure of psychological and spiritual values that define who we are and how we are going to live. New meaning must be found for our lives, and this whole challenging and often painful process must become a meaningful experience in its own right. My discussions of outrageous courage, compassion, and love are meant as guides for developing restructured personal foundations and, I hope, for the restructuring of our social character.

Now let us look more closely at our society's current apocalypse and attempt to better understand it as an archetypal process that we are in the middle of experiencing, and being turned upside down by. But first let us again briefly define an apocalypse. It is a devastating event or series of events. An apocalypse challenges us to see the destruction of our worldview, of the psychological and spiritual value structures that have supported our identity, of the persona we present to others, and of the way we live in the world. It forces us to face what we experience as terrible truths as it reveals to us not only our shadows but also our lack of awareness, our denial, and our repression of all that we are and have been. We also face the choice Price did: let the old die in order to embrace new life—one in which our power instinct and our love instinct are balanced—or sink into despair and become the victims of fate.

—— ••• ——

Thoughts and Questions to Ponder

Facing reality and accepting it are generally thought of as the first steps toward healing, growth, problem solving, and creating positive change. All of these require an accurate understanding of reality. Too often, though, we are unaware that understanding reality is no simple task. What do you think of the statement, "Self-awareness and growing consciousness are crucial because, no matter what we think, we all live in a self-inflicted condition of limited awareness of reality"?

How has the discussion of our early experiences' influence on our worldview and our response to events expanded your understanding of our perception of reality?

Does it make sense to you that for us to accurately understand reality, we first have to develop an accurate understanding of ourselves and the forces that have shaped and directed us? My books *Sacred Selfishness* and *Becoming Whole* are devoted to this task.

How does the following statement affect you, "If we don't become aware of our dominant complexes, we will always be susceptible to outside manipulation on many levels"?

Other Thoughts?

———— •✦• ————

UNDERSTANDING THIS APOCALYPSE

An apocalypse, as I have noted, is an event or series of events that stop our lives dead in their tracks. It is accompanied by passionate emotional intensity because of the powerful effect it has on us. An apocalypse can be individual, societal, or even global in scope. It is an explosion of the life force into our lives in a conscious realization of that force. In his book *Archetype of the Apocalypse*, Dr. Edward F. Edinger breaks the archetype of the apocalypse down into four components:

1. Revelation
2. Judgement
3. Destruction or Punishment
4. A New World

Let us look closely at and briefly explain the first three components and describe how some of our experiences correlate with them.

The first element, **Revelation**, brings a shattering new insight into our personal and collective lives. This insight threatens our identity: the structure of our personalities, the way we are living and have envisioned the future, and our sense of safety now and into the future.

The 2016 presidential campaign and election began a series of such shocking revelations. It seemed that even the new president and the people who voted for him were shocked by the outcome of the election. Many more people were bewildered by the deep and, for the most part, previously unseen anger that was revealed in such a large number of our citizens. They were also shocked by the passionate desire of so many people to destroy our society's status quo and many of its institutions and to give license to some of our baser instincts. Brutality, White supremacy, misogyny, and the naked quest for power (though it often seemed misdirected and self-destructive) emerged as seemingly accepted themes.

Without realizing it, we appeared to have lost authority over the narrative sides of our own lives. There no longer seemed to be a coherent sense of substantial identity or citizenship in our society. Consequently, our personal sense of "I" was no longer safe and reliable, nor was our future. Many people in our society turned to an authority figure to give them their sense of a societal "I" and resisted having that "identity" threatened in any way.

In 2020 the COVID-19 pandemic revealed our inability to come together and face a national crisis in a manner so staggering I could never have imagined it. It has confronted us with devastating disaster and challenges that bring into question our national character, as well as our concerns for each other, humanity, and the future.

The second component Edinger gives us is **Judgement**. In fact, this aspect of an apocalypse is a continuing revelation, an "unmasking" of a reality that has been there growing all the time but that we have not seen clearly before. This unveiling is a very humbling experience that bursts the bubbles of illusion we have been living in. If we can marshal the courage, we will learn in a new way that our actions have consequences; when we sought to live in comfort and isolation from true reality, we built up a huge backlash that is now hitting us. It is crucially important for us to realize that each one of these abrupt, profound revelations is a question the life force is requiring us to face.

Edinger points out that the abrupt, profound revelation of our personal and/or collective shadow can be overpowering enough to threaten complete demoralization. He writes that when we are confronted with our personal and/or our collective dark and dubious nature—which we have known only abstractly and intellectually, or have stayed willfully unaware of—it comes as a big shock. I will share with you several revelations that I also have known abstractly and intellectually, some of which I even experienced personally and have written about, that were nevertheless stunning to me. And I am astounded that collectively we have paid so little attention to them.

This period of time has certainly focused national attention on the horrible, brutal history of racism in our country. It also revealed that racism is very present today, is institutionalized, and continues to be denied and upheld on many fronts.

At its founding our country created a brutal social and economic caste system that has rigidified in the last fifty years. The institutionalization of income disparity has trapped so many Americans in economic desperation that it now makes what we thought of as "America, the land of opportunity" a cruel fiction.

In my book *The Midnight Hour: A Jungian Perspective on America's Pivotal Moment*, I titled the chapter on healthcare, "Healthcare: Isn't It Time to Quit Being the Cruelest Developed Nation?" The pandemic has underlined this point, and we still have, particularly for nonpandemic illnesses, the most uncaring and most expensive healthcare system of any developed nation.

Our ability to be civil to one another seems absolutely shipwrecked. The bitter political and factional disputes, even in our own families, illustrate the climate of chaos we are living in. The rage that bursts out in public events and the fanatical political action groups—not only at war with each other but also energizing the impetus for us to see one another as enemies—are traumatizing us daily.

Our democratic institutions seem to be threatened as never before. There has been a ruthless takeover of the democratic levels of our government by ultrawealthy families, rich corporations, and highly funded special interest groups, all of which are interested in their own power and welfare.

Further, there is an incredible resistance to a total commitment to counter climate change, which is rapidly on the way to causing a worldwide holocaust.

Again, I must mention my total shock at how the pandemic, though it revealed some heroes, has more dramatically shown the lack of a national character structure that can unite us in confronting our most difficult challenges as we have in the past.

Another thing that brought me to my knees is the in-your-face loss of the sacredness of individual lives. We allow horrible, violent deaths to become banal factors in our news cycles: Black lives ended carelessly, numerous victims of mass shootings, over 93,000 opioid deaths in a year, over 700,000 COVID deaths as of this writing. These are all horrible ways to die, full of suffering, devastating to families, friends, and communities. Yet I use the words "banal factors in our news cycles" because, for the most part, we have become "onlookers" and not roused, active citizens demanding change.

We have experienced these revelations daily with no seeming end or solution in sight. You may be able to think of more things you have experienced than I have listed. But as I am thinking about them, I am reminded of the Dark Night of the Soul in the mystic's journey to know the Divine. Fear—often despair, suffering, and fatigue—permeate the lives of the people I know and consult with. This is a Dark Night of the Soul for our social character. This unveiling is frightening, painful, and humiliating. But this forced awareness should begin the discovery of much that is really troubling us and our nation and should be very valuable to the new person and society we are now called to create.

The third component Edinger presents is one he calls the theme of **Destruction** or **Punishment**. Destruction happens when we are individually seized by fear and anxiety in the midst of the demand for transformation. We are particularly seized by fear because the previous values of our social character—positive thinking, achievement, economic and material success—no longer answer the challenges we face today. In addition, the current structure of our social character devalues and actually fears any attempt to look at ourselves and our society with insight and emotional honesty. In our current state our collective response to the symptoms of the apocalypse fall primarily into three defensive patterns: fight, flight, or freeze. These are typical responses to strong feelings of anxiety.

The easiest defense mechanism to see is the "fight" choice. People who choose this response are also in denial. As I pointed out before, this response seeks a feeling of empowerment by means of an aggressive, angry stance that covers an unconscious fear of vulnerability and helplessness. The causes of this deep underlying fear are projected onto other people, groups, and institutions. All too often, when taking this stance, we defend against the possibility of experiencing pain by causing pain in others we are projecting our negativity onto. We project the causes of the pain we have repressed into our shadows because we are unable or unwilling to face reality. Then we begin to see these people, groups of people, and institutions as evil enemies. Politicians and the media have learned how to manipulate the unconscious fear that drives this kind of anger very well. Choosing the path of anger and aggression is also making the choice to be willfully ignorant of reality. Unfortunately, choosing this path to deal with anxiety generally begins a process of accelerating it and rigidifying the people choosing this response.

The second common defense mechanism or response to fear and intense anxiety is "flight," and flight's most common form is denial. We take flight as we unconsciously screen out realities that threaten our self-image, our emotional safety, our value systems, and our preferred view of the world. We turn away from unpleasant sights, topics of conversation, or behavior. It is easier to have no time to acknowledge challenging personal and social problems, using the excuse we are so preoccupied with work, responsibilities, obligations, family problems, and so on. We may also use the excuse that we are too sensitive and vulnerable to face the pain around us. People choosing this response are also being willfully ignorant of reality.

The third common way of responding to threat and anxiety is to "freeze" and attempt to stay willfully naive. This choice isn't quite as obvious as the first two but it is also common. It reminds me of a comment the well-known writer James Baldwin made in an interview in 1961. He said, "Most of us, no matter what we say, are walking in the dark, whistling in the dark." I might call our whistling rationalizing. We cover our freezing with rationalizations. Of course, our media, our entertainment industry, and general culture don't help us be honest with ourselves. We have rationalized violence. Even when it is in our face, we quickly seek to get past it without really seeking to understand its sources and to then take action. We have rationalized cheating, stealing, and lying, especially in business and politics. We have rationalized greed and the pursuit of "the good life" based on materialism. Being frozen beneath the surface of our lives is not just an expression of helplessness. It is also an expression of hopelessness.

———— •✦• ————

We can easily see that an apocalypse is living it-self out in our society and the world. In psycholog-ical terms this means "in the collective psyche, in an unconscious and therefore destructive way." The collective Self, the life force, challenges us directly to consciously awaken to the brutal realities that it reveals and that we have tried so hard to avoid. We must remember Jung's statement that what we haven't faced in ourselves and life will become our fate. The truth is, as it always is, that when facing our shadow and our own darkness, whether per-sonal or collective, we must not get bogged down in discouragement, guilt, or shame. What is called for is the response Price describes: "Have one hard cry, if the tears will come. Then stanch the grief, by whatever legal means. Next find your way to be somebody else, the next viable you—a stripped-down whole other clear-eyed person, realistic as a sawed-off shotgun, and thankful for air."

Understanding the archetype of the apocalypse, as Edinger so carefully explains it, is important be-cause archetypes function as conduits for our in-stinctual energy, meaning the life forces within us. Jung says they are like a "dry riverbed" that will channel the energy when it comes. Archetypal ener-gy can flow in either positive or negative directions, depending upon how conscious we are of their presence and power—and our resulting choice. The apocalypse confronts us with a reality that challenges us to create a whole new character structure, within ourselves and our society, that changes the foundation and direction from power to love.

For several generations, we have breathed in like air the values of material success and positive thinking. These values have become foundational in our social character. They have become pillars supporting our often unconscious quest for power. When Jung says, "Where love stops, power begins, and violence, and terror," we are challenged to reverse our course toward power, violence, and terror and to renew love as the foundation that supports our lives. The renewal of courage, love, and compassion must be the bedrock supporting a "whole new life" for us. To not make this choice will lead to increasing deaths and disasters.

— ◦│◦ —

Thoughts and Questions to Ponder

As you explore more about the psychological meaning of this apocalypse and what it reveals about our lives, our reality, and our world, are you gaining a better understanding of the reality you and the rest of us are facing?

Can you think of and list in your journal several instances when the shock of unveiling the dark sides of our society has prompted your fight, flight, or freeze mentality? How do you see these reactions taking place around you?

Does understanding the apocalypse better bring new meaning for you to Jung's statement, "Where love stops, power begins, and violence, and terror"? Studying the structure of the apocalypse from Edinger's perspective and applying this structure to the situation we are experiencing is challenging and discouraging.

Do you think that Price's advice directing us to a whole new life gives us hope? Is it helpful to you to remember these words of Nelson Mandela, "It always seems impossible until it's done," or those of the great poet Theodore Roethke, "What we need is more people who specialize in the impossible"?

Other Thoughts?

PART III

————·•·————

Initiating a Whole New Life

"Everything good is costly, and the development of personality is one of the most costly of all things. It is a matter of saying yes to ourself, of taking oneself as the most serious of tasks, of being conscious of everything one does, and keeping it constantly before one's eyes in all its dubious aspects—truly a task that taxes us to the utmost.

". . . The individual must devote himself to the way with all his energy, for it is only by means of his integrity that he can go further, and his integrity alone can guarantee that his way will not turn out to be an absurd misadventure."

—*Carl Jung*

CULTIVATING OUTRAGEOUS COURAGE

In my various writings I have often described my father as a storm-driven man. Coming from a common background, he boldly stepped into the challenging struggles of life, education, marriage, the Great Depression, a world war—a life of trials. He was driven by courage and desperation. Our relationship was passionate and conflictual. But I miss him. His spirit, passion, desperation, and courage flow through my veins.

I have spent a lot of time during my life thinking about passion, desperation, and courage. It is clear to me why, many centuries ago, Aristotle asserted that courage is the most important virtue: without it we can't practice any of the others. Courage is the nearest star, casting the light that energizes our growth. The great poet, educator, and humanitarian Maya Angelou says that we must be courageous about facing our personal histories, that we must find the courage to care and to create internally as well as externally. And, as she says, we need courage "to create ourselves daily as Christians, as Jews, as Muslims, as thinking, caring, laughing, loving human beings."

As an analyst, I have been concerned for decades

by our society's dwindling of courage, its polarization of aggression, and its disregard for the daily choice of good over evil. We seem to have lost sight of the lofty expanse of our founding documents. Instead, the focus has narrowed to a shallow version of the "pursuit of happiness," and the rationale for our behavior has become pragmatic, problem solving, and conflict oriented. In politics, business, and our personal lives, many of us have become "players" or "onlookers" rather than having the courage to be full participants. As a result, our sense of right and wrong seems to be fading away, and we are losing the ability to act with courage and resolve toward the major problems and threats in our own front yard.

Courage in its fullest sense becomes a **foundation** when we open ourselves to experiencing life and ourselves in their wholeness. Love, loyalty, living creatively, living our authentic values, caring for ourselves and others all require taking risks, and such risks call for courage of the heart. The word *courage* comes from the French word *coeur*, which means "heart." It is courage that pumps the life force throughout our being. Below are seven principles that are necessary to help us understand the more profound meanings of courage and that can guide our development of it every day.

1. Have the courage to honor fear. Fear is an important part of our nature. Fear is a dragon we have to face again and again in a life that we are living wholeheartedly. Just as we find other strong feelings, or even illnesses, are the seeds for our growth, the same is true for fear. It takes outrageous courage to accept the fear within ourselves. We must learn not to repress it, deny it, or look for the easiest way out. It speaks to something important within or outside of us, and that leads us to my second principle. But, before reading on, you might take some time and ask yourself this question: As you were growing up, how were you taught to deal with fear, and how do you deal with it now?

2. Have the courage to understand fear. If we fail to understand our fears and their origins, they will become a mounting force in our unconscious that will constantly undermine our self-confidence, our abilities to face needed changes and growth, and our ability to appreciate ourselves and opportunities to enjoy life. Seeking to understand fear doesn't mean to embrace or give in to it. Fear is seductive, and if we allow it to unconsciously drive us, we can become seduced by the false gods of achievement, money, security, appearances, magical others, and magical leaders. Keep in mind that understanding fear is a spiritual journey because it is so easy to quickly sell ourselves out in the face of fear. Journaling about your efforts to understand the force of fear in yourself and in our society is an effective and rewarding way to challenge the worldview you actually live by.

3. Have the courage to let yourself live with fear. The truth is that life is difficult. If we choose to be fully alive, we must have the courage to take risks and encounter unforeseen challenges. This is reality, even though we seek the illusion that a well-planned, carefully lived, good life will be unburdened by troubles. But neither God nor Buddha nor any other great spiritual leader or tradition guarantees or even encourages a trouble-free life. In fact, attempting to keep that illusion can contribute to the arrival of an apocalypse. Throughout history our great spiritual figures inspire us to grow through our painful experiences by seeking to understand their lessons. Although we may think it is safer to avoid trouble than to seek it, trouble often ends up finding us anyway. Remember, courage means acting, loving, and being compassionate even when we are afraid. Without fear, courage is meaningless.

4. We need courage to create. Whether we are creating art, a new business, or a new life, we need rage and passion to break out of the chrysalis of fear, pride, conventional thinking, our need for approval, our misguided value structure, or whatever is encapsulating us. Creativity requires the courage to concentrate all of our passion, our love, our anger, our rage, and our hatred combined with our sensitivity and our thoughtfulness.

When rage and hate are destructively acted out, they may be wasted, they may be a defensive outlet, and they may be creativity gone wrong. Or they may be an apocalyptic symbol. You might ask yourself if you have a bias toward rage that keeps you from realizing its positive and symbolic value.

5. **Have the courage to listen to your shadow.** Our shadows are those parts of ourselves that we have repressed, denied, and rejected into our unconscious. They are, or we fear they would be, socially unacceptable, shameful, threatening, embarrassing; we have put some of our potentials in these categories because we are afraid that if we tried to accept them, they would take us out of our comfort and safety zones. We might see them as symbolized by enemies, beggars, thieves, prisoners, diseased people, strangers, and so on in our dreams. In fact, in real life it is the disenfranchised people, the alienated people who can tell us the truth about what is wrong in our society. The same is true in our inner society, and we must have the courage to get to know these parts of ourselves so we can understand the unconscious structure that governs our lives. This is a very important point to think about. Both personally and as a society, we tend to prefer willful ignorance over finding the outrageous courage to face the painful realities we are creating. To face the truth about our shadows and reconcile with them

personally and societally is the path to a new structure of values, meaning, and purpose. The path begins with courage.

6. We need courage to honor the individuation instinct. To choose life is to choose individuation. For Jung, our most basic instinct is the instinct for developing consciousness, the instinct for individuation—in other words, the instinctual life force calling for the complete development of our full potential. Honoring that instinct requires outrageous courage because it entails a lifelong process of psychospiritual life, death, and rebirth. Individuation confronts us with conflicts, life events, and situations that call for us to challenge ourselves, to see reality in new ways, and to recreate ourselves and our worldview. It takes courage to choose life and give up safety and comfort as signs of spiritual and material success. I accept it as a challenge that still comes as a shock but is reality in its most rewarding sense.

7. We need courage to love and be vulnerable. Love demands courage because it always makes us open to pain and loss. A love of life opens us to the sufferings of life. But denying or trying to avoid and escape such suffering has two other consequences. First, according to Jung, the effort to ward off true suffering is what created neurotic suffering. Second, if we close the door on suffering, we close the door on real joy. For many years in our society, the pursuit of a kind of driven happiness has been the theme. As a result, we are a society with very little knowledge of joy. To love in a substantial way requires courage because it leads us to the full experience of being human. It takes outrageous courage to love the light within ourselves, the potential to love.

— ❖ —

The apocalypse we are living through is the death of an age. It is up to us to midwife the birth of a new age, and if we fail at this task, we will see the destructive aspects of the apocalypse increase dramatically. Shall we, as we feel our foundations quaking, retreat into fear, despair, or indifference? Or shall we try to cover our deepest fears with angry outbursts and tribal wars? If we do, we will have abandoned our duties to ourselves, to those we love and care about, to humanity, and to the future. If we do, we will have turned our backs on the teachings of our greatest religions. If we do, we will have forsaken the American ideals of freedom, equality, and liberty. If we do, we will have relinquished *hope*, which is grounded in a person's and a community's ability to work for something because it is good.

Or shall we seize the courage necessary to renew our personal and collective values of the heart—sensitivity, caring for one another, awareness, and responsibility—in the face of radical challenges? Shall we, through strengthening ourselves, building our awareness, and broadening our understanding, participate in forming a new social character for our country?

We are called upon in the midst of an apocalypse to destroy the old and to create new selves and a new society and to right many old wrongs we have experienced or perpetuated personally and collectively. We are being called and pushed into new territories where there are no well-worn paths; no one has been there before and returned to guide us. To commit to "a whole new life" is to live into the future by stepping into the unknown, and because there is no road map to reassure us, this requires outrageous courage.

Courage opens doors to hope, to an orientation of the spirit, to the imagination, to love in all of its complexities, and it sees beyond the horizon.

————— ◦✦◦ —————

Thoughts and Questions to Ponder

How seriously have you thought about courage during your life? Have you generally, like most of us, thought it was simply being brave in dangerous situations? Have you, like most of us, thought it means not having fear?

What does my statement that "courage in its fullest sense becomes a foundation when we open ourselves to experiencing life and ourselves in their wholeness. Love, loyalty, living creatively, caring for ourselves and others all require taking risks, and such risks call for courage of the heart," bring to mind for you? Does it stir your feelings?

Were you surprised when you read, "Have the courage to honor fear," "Have the courage to understand fear," "Have the courage to let yourself live with fear"?

How did you respond when you read, "We need courage to create. Whether we are creating art, a new business, or a new life, we need rage and passion to break out of the chrysalis of fear, pride, conventional thinking, our need for approval, our misguided value structure, or whatever is encapsulating us"? What are some ways you have built up rigid structures that now limit your vigorous and creative response to the readings, to aspects of the apocalypse we are experiencing, or to your own life situations? Are these structures affecting your responses right now?

It might be helpful for you to journal a personal response to each one of the seven principles in this section on courage and the ones coming up on love and compassion.

As you reflect on this section about cultivating outrageous courage, what do you feel about commitment to a whole new life?

Other Thoughts?

———— •◆• ————

CULTIVATING OUTRAGEOUS LOVE

One–The Healing Power of Self-Love

As I opened this book, I included two quotations from Jung that have confronted me for decades. The first one is, "Where love stops, power begins, and violence, and terror." The second one is that "the individual's feeling of weakness, indeed of non-existence, was thus compensated by the eruption of hitherto unknown desires for power." These statements are ever present in the back of my mind as I reflect on the apocalypse we are in.

Not long ago I was rereading *The Fire Next Time* by James Baldwin. It had been years since I first read it. As I was being drawn back into it, page 22 actually, I read these sentences: "White people in this country will have quite enough to do in learning how to accept and love themselves and each other, and when they have achieved this—which will not be tomorrow and may very well be never—the Negro problem will no longer exist, for it will no longer be needed."

I was stunned to read these sentences. This is one of the most profound passages I have ever read. In a few sentences he shifts the ground of our racial

problems and the responsibility of White people
into a challenge I had never thought of and whose
truth is beyond dispute. He also challenges African
Americans to love themselves in a similar way.

Two thousand years ago a revolutionary called
Jesus gave us a great commandment, the second part
of which is to "love your neighbor as yourself." We
have paid a heavy price throughout history for not
learning what this simple sounding but incredibly
profound commandment means if we seek to live
by it. When I was young, I thought self-love was the
most natural thing in the world. But it is not. With
maturity, I learned better. Self-interest and self-denial may seem natural, but they are more likely driven
by our complexes and wounded hearts. Self-love is
another story. Self-love is one of the most difficult
things in the world to achieve. This commandment
in a simply straightforward way challenges us to a
series of quests that are demanding and yet promise
more than we can easily imagine. Jung, as I quoted
him earlier, explains where failure in these quests
leads us. Baldwin outlines the promise of these
quests when self-love becomes the foundation for
mediating our relationships.

I remember very well when the idea that Jesus's
commandment directs people to love themselves in
order to love their neighbor became very popular
and widely discussed. This encounter with what it
might mean to love myself was in the early 1970s.

When it came right down to it, I realized I didn't have a very good idea of how to love myself. At the time I was just starting graduate school, and we were studying the works of the great humanistic psychologist Dr. Carl Rogers. Rogers taught that the ingredients for a healing and growth-sustaining therapeutic relationship were to be genuinely engaged in the relationship, to be emotionally congruent in it, to be emotionally warm in it, to be empathetic and understanding in it, and to give the other person "unconditional positive regard." Well, I concluded, if I don't really know what it means to love myself, it won't hurt to try to have a good therapeutic relationship with myself since I'm studying how to do this with other people anyway. So, I began reviewing these steps nightly in my journal and practicing them on myself. I particularly like the idea of giving myself unconditional positive regard. I have always thought the idea of unconditional love is infantilizing, and I wanted my self-love to be strengthening. This practice had a profound effect on me and, I believe, on my development as a therapist all those decades ago.

Self-love, in its fullest sense, becomes a burning necessity when we open ourselves to our wholeness. It becomes the foundation not only of our love of life but also of the family of humanity and its future. I want to share with you seven principles that I have used in my lectures and books that

are necessary to open the door to self-love one day
at a time.

1. **Remember, love is difficult,** the poet Rainer Ma-
ria Rilke explains, in contrast to the sentimental
way we like to think about it. Review your thoughts
about love. Do you think it should just bring happiness, ease, or at least security? Do explosions, struggles, and failures make you think love has failed?
Life isn't easy and love can't be easy either.

2. **Cultivating self-love is an odyssey with moments
of difficulty and joy.** It's an excursion into knowing
ourselves, into asking whether what we are doing is
adding to or diminishing our feelings of self-worth.

3. **Self-love challenges boundaries that we have
fenced ourselves into such as practicality, conventional wisdom, and other people's perspectives.** We
must gently ask ourselves whose voice we are really
hearing in our head. Is it the voice of our heart or
something bigger, like our true Self?

4. **Self-love isn't self-indulgent.** It isn't shopping
sprees, outlandish vacations, sneaking sweets, or pou-
ting moods. It is the commitment to growing in self-
knowledge and in our capacity to love. Remember,
taking the time for reflection isn't egocentric. It is
the key to having the kind of vitality that overflows.

5. **Self-love is the foundation that determines how
strongly we can give and receive love.** Without it,
our relationships will crumble under the slightest

storm. Take the responsibility for understanding your fears and needs, and for facing them in a loving way.

6. Self-love rests on self-forgiveness. It entails being able to understand who we were when we failed ourselves and what needs, hurts, fears, and deprivations were driving us. Only then may we meet ourselves with compassion and kindness. This is why our growth in self-understanding brings healing and reconciliation with our essential selves.

7. Self-love is learning how to be tough with ourselves. It is the ability to take the driver's seat in our life when we need to break a destructive mood or habit. We must remember that being tough with ourselves means being committed and energetic, having high standards and tenacity. Being tough with ourselves is the opposite of being hard on ourselves, which means being perfectionistic, self-critical, self-punishing, and unaccepting of our mistakes and weaknesses. It is important for us to remember each day that to embody love, to be love, begins with a foundation of self-love and self-compassion.

Love, as you can easily imagine from reading these steps, takes courage. As the pandemic and economic and political chaos keep staring us in the face, we must remember that, throughout history, having courage of the heart is one of our noblest virtues. Facing this journey we have been thrust into, we must turn it into a quest by having the courage to learn and seek. Even if we become seekers as a result of desperation, we can and must find courage within ourselves, because it is so easy to fall into despair, bitterness, and helplessness in the face of our difficulties.

Courage enables us to look into the darkness in our lives, in ourselves and to search for the light of new meaning, new purpose, and new directions, as well as the path to grow beyond our current situation. When we love ourselves, when we feel the love and support deep within us, we find the courage and the energy to imagine new things, new lives. The experience of being loved creates in us the desire to be transformed. We undergo a softening toward and an increased awareness of others. And we must remember that love always takes the risk of birth, no matter what state the world is in.

In the end of *The Fire Next Time*, Baldwin imagined that relatively conscious Whites and relatively conscious people of color could lovingly create new consciousness in others and change the trajectory of the world. And, he said, we must dare everything. True self-love is the foundation of outrageous love that gives hope, purpose, and direction to a reimagined future and the courage to dare everything for it.

——— •∤• ———

Thoughts and Questions to Ponder

While you were reading this section, I shared with you that "when I was young, I thought self-love was the most natural thing in the world. But it is not. With maturity, I learned better. Self-interest and self-denial may seem natural, but they are more likely driven by our complexes and wounded hearts. Self-love is another story. Self-love is one of the most difficult things in the world to achieve." Can you make a list of all of the ways you find self-love hard to achieve?

What do you think of my using Rogers's approach to the therapeutic relationship—being genuinely engaged, emotionally congruent, warm, and sympathetic, as well as unconditional positive regard—as the first steps on my own path to self-love?

As you read these principles and reflect on them, respond to each one by writing in your journal.

What does it mean to you that "love always takes the risk of birth, no matter what state the world is in"? It may be helpful to reread the next-to-last paragraph in this section, which ends with the above reminder.

Other Thoughts?

Two–Love Must Be Strong

Love is strong, must be recognized as strong; it must be willing to roar. Analyst Dr. James Hillman writes in *The Thought of the Heart and the Soul of the World* that when young lions are born, they must be awakened with a roar. He tells us the young lions need to be awakened in our hearts. He writes, "What is passive, immobile, asleep in the heart creates a desert which can only be cured by its own parenting principle that shows its awakening care by roaring. . . . The more our desert, the more we must rage, which rage is love." These thoughts leave me wondering, "Can we ever again become wholly what we are meant to be?"

For years, all my writing has sought to understand what is happening to our society, to us and to me. I believe my first task is to see and accept reality. Then I must seek to understand it from a personal perspective. Failing to understand the truth of our experiences individually and collectively is the surest guarantee of increasing strife that will assault the well-being of every one of us. Failing to understand the challenges we face will cause us to pay a dear price in our innermost lives as well as in the spirit of our country. I think I have made it clear throughout that facing our reality and seeking to understand it does not mean that we take on an attitude of permitting or acquiescing to anything.

Accepting and understanding reality is the necessary foundation that will help us face the apocalypse we are in today, create a whole new life for ourselves and our society, and quit paying the price of our ignorance in blood.

My reflections bring to mind a talk that Dr. Philip Hallie gave titled "Cruelty: The Empirical Evil" at a symposium on "Facing Evil" (in a book with the same title) put together by Jungian analyst Dr. Harry Wilmer in the mid-1980s. Hallie was a well-known author and the Griffin Professor of Philosophy and Humanities at Wesleyan University in Middletown, Connecticut. A World War II veteran, he became intrigued with the story of Le Chambon, a small French mountain village that devoted itself during the war to rescuing refugees from the Nazis—at the risk of the villagers' lives. Hallie was so moved by this story that he incorporated it into a book that became an international best seller. At the time, the village exemplified for Hallie the power of love.

But, as time passed, he began to feel that something in his heart resented this village. He said, "They didn't stop Hitler. They did nothing to stop Hitler. . . . A thousand Le Chambons would not have stopped Hitler. It took decent murderers like me to do it. Murderers who had compunctions, but murdered nonetheless. . . . The cruelty that I perpetrated willingly was the only way to stop the cruel march that I and others like me were facing." Hallie received three Battle Stars while serving with the famous Eighty-Second Airborne Division in Europe during World War II.

Hallie's story reminds me that the great social psychoanalyst Erich Fromm, in his book *The Anatomy of Human Destructiveness*, defined two kinds of aggression: malignant and benign. Malignant aggression destroys life. Benign aggression is used in the service of life. When we are called to face the malignant aggression in our lives—in our politics, our society, our cities, our families, and within ourselves—it is a call to use a force of will, assertion, and commitment. In other words, we must use the power of the outrageous love of life against the forces destroying life. We are in this world to be healers, listeners, servants, and lovers. We are also here to be creators and spiritual warriors.

A few years ago, there was a lot of social discourse about people living in a bubble. In too many cases, too many of us had remained conveniently ignorant of cruelties in our society, and some of us even regarded this ignorance as a virtue. On many levels we experienced innocent naivete, or willful naivete. Consequently, we neither saw nor understood the cruelty we were personally and collectively participating in. In fact, I now consider willful naivete and willful ignorance to be malicious aggression because they destroy life-affirming opportunities at both the individual and the societal level. In every chapter in my book *The Midnight Hour*, I am straightforward about the cruelties in our society to people all around us, and even to ourselves, that we need to wake up to.

The people who scare me the most are the "good people." The ones theologian Reinhold Niebuhr was referring to when he said, "Most evil is not done by evil people, but by good people who don't know what they are doing." Good people who are willfully naive may attend religious services, give money to charities, collect clothes for people who are homeless, spend their holidays serving food to people who are food insecure. "Good people" decry violence, listen to impassioned sermons, go to adult forums and lectures on spirituality. But here are the real questions: Will they do anything to change the dark issues revealed in our apocalypse? Will they step out of their comfort zones and imagined security to stop the predators trying to take over our government? In his great book *The Strength to Love*, Martin Luther King Jr. warned us that sincerity and conscientiousness are not enough. Will they/we/I love life enough to become outrageously fierce in the service of life?

Unfortunately, people who were raised in the White pseudo-Christian middle-class, as I was, were taught prejudices that are great stumbling blocks to the ability to be aggressive in the service of life. We were trained to be *nice*, to avoid anger, not to mention acting in anger (much less in outrage). We were even taught that expressing ourselves clearly and directly is being aggressive or confrontational. In essence, we were taught that to be kind and loving is to be passive and pleasing.

We need to awaken and love life dearly. As I write these words, I am reminded of a story I've used in my books and lectures. It is an old story of Saint Francis and the wolf that has helped me develop a sense of comfort, even affection, with the savage side of myself. The story takes place a long time ago when there were still vast forests in Italy. The people in a small village began to notice that some of their chickens and livestock were disappearing. Then, tragically, some children and older people went missing. As the villagers put together a few clues—bloody bits of fur, signs of struggles, and paw prints—they realized a ferocious wolf had moved into the nearby woods.

Animals and weaker people were customary prey, but the wolf seemed to be getting increasingly bolder. The villagers tried in vain to poison, capture, or kill the wolf, but they were unable to even find it. They called for hunters from near and far to kill it. Elegant nobles with great horses, packs of hounds, and many retainers tried to help the villagers. But the wolf evaded them all.

Eventually the village elders, in desperation, sent a message to Saint Francis. Saint Francis came immediately to their aid. He arrived at the village and plunged into the forest, without pausing to eat or rest. He journeyed deeper into the dense vegetation than anyone had before, searching for the wolf's lair. In the twilight of a small clearing, he found the wolf. They stood before each other, eye to eye, for some time. Finally, Saint Francis said simply, "Brother wolf."

When Saint Francis returned to the village, the excited people gathered around him and begged him to tell them how to deal with the wolf. He said to them, "Feed your wolf." The lesson is simple. We must face our capacity for fierceness. Feeding our capacity for fierceness means honoring it with conscious awareness and integrating it into our personalities as part of our journey into wholeness. Feeding our wolf is necessary to give us the strength not only to support a life of love and responsibility but also to respond to personal and social problems with caring and competence—responses that honor our tradition of human dignity, the sacredness of each person, and our ideal of a community in which people help one another.

We need to learn that outrageous love is strong. Outrageous love must have strength, purpose, and direction. Outrageous love must be passionate and creative. Love, in its most authentic form, tells us that allowing our current national condition of cruelty under the guise of not being "aggressive" is a form of extremism that will disgrace us in the eyes of our children and grandchildren—in the eyes of history as well as the future.

This type of love requires sacrifice, meaning that we must learn to love the lives of others as well as our own. This type of love makes it clear that comfort can quickly become its own corruption. When we love beyond our own lives and comfort, we begin to love the lives of those connected to us, and we are challenged and inspired to build a better world for all of us.

When we don't confront reality and the cruelties being inflicted by our societal shadows, we set ourselves up to pay a terrible price. If we don't personally and collectively embrace the changes we need to make for the evolution of our consciousness and social awareness, I believe the price we pay will be in blood. Jung also believed this, as illustrated in his writings in *Civilization in Transition* (CW, vol. 10), and Hallie expresses this in his writings as well. In fact, we have paid this price in blood for some time. However, if we do take the risks and face the challenges of change and transformation that are clearly beckoning us, we will invite the breath of life to renew us and to open our minds, hearts, and lives to a whole new life together. Loving authentically means using every single means at our disposal to pursue and enhance our values of life, liberty, opportunity, equality, and justice for all.

As you can likely see, writing these words brings into focus for me the fact that outrageous love demands clarity, passion, and action. Yet, I still wonder if I have written enough.

—— ⋅⧫⋅ ——

Thoughts and Questions to Ponder

Love must be strong. Love must be willing to roar. Love must be as fierce as a wolf; love must be willing to fight for life and must exist in the service of life. Write out for yourself how these descriptions of love match up with how you were taught to define love and a loving life.

What was your response to my statement that denial in the form of willful naivete and ignorance are malicious aggression because they destroy the life-affirming opportunities for individuals and for society?

Did it make sense to you when you read, "The people who scare me the most are the 'good people'"?

Can you list comforts that have become corruptions in your life?

Can you now write a summary of what strong love means to you?

Other Thoughts?

CULTIVATING OUTRAGEOUS COMPASSION

*R*evitalizing compassion is an interesting term to me. To revitalize means to take something that is deteriorating and inject new life into it. The true definition of *compassion* is "to suffer with" or "to suffer together." Well, while I was brought up to think being compassionate is a virtue, I was taught practically nothing about what it might mean besides empathy or pity. Of course, empathy and pity are not suffering with or feeling with. Empathy or pity all too often bring no real understanding of the life experiences and circumstances of the other person or group of people.

The well-known religious writer Karen Armstrong tells us in her memoir, *The Spiral Staircase: My Climb Out of Darkness*, that she discovered that "the theme of compassion . . . is pivotal to all of the great religious traditions . . . at their best." I have been in and out of churches for decades and have not encountered compassion, "suffering with," as a central theme in their Sunday teachings. Yet, as I have read the New Testament, it seems to me that to feed the hungry, give drink to the thirsty, welcome the stranger, clothe the naked, visit the sick, and write to the prisoner are in some form the general theme in every sermon of Jesus. Further, he says in Mathew 25:20, "I tell you solemnly, in so far as you did this to the least of these brothers (and sisters) of mine you did it to me." With these words he makes compassion a sacred activity. I wonder what has happened to those of us who call ourselves Christians and how we can all begin to become what our great religions are calling us to become.

Jung gives us the starting point for revitalizing the strength of compassion within ourselves. In *Collected Works* (vol. 11, par. 520–521), he writes that accepting ourselves with compassion is the first journey we must make. This point of view puts a whole new slant on how we were taught about compassion in the past. It challenges us in a more personal and profound way. We must suffer with ourselves, seek out the beggar, the infirm, the enemy, the stranger, and the criminal within ourselves. We must not preach but reflect. We must seek out the parts of ourselves we condemn, rage against, hide from the world, and deny from our awareness. We must be able to "give them the alms of our own kindness," seek not to embrace them but to understand them with compassion. This course brings true humility to us, and as this journey continues, we learn more about how to live with wisdom and the practice of inner compassion flows outward.

In my lectures and writings, I have described this approach to the journey of cultivating compassion as the "Descent into Life." When I have written and spoken about this journey, I've always found it interesting, even amusing, that when the newest pied piper for enlightenment is speaking in our town, he or she is usually focusing on how we can achieve peace and joy. Well, no wonder! That is what sells and what creates followings because that is what so many of us think we are longing for.

On the other hand, as Armstrong points out, all of our great religions (and I am not speaking of the pied pipers they also have), those that religious scholar Huston Smith calls our wisdom traditions, have a very different emphasis. For example, a rabbi famous in Jewish history lived in a tent pitched next to the walls of Jerusalem because he wanted to be close to the poor. When Siddhārtha walked out of his father's palace, he came face-to-face with poverty, illness, and death. These encounters launched his journey into becoming the Buddha. In Christianity, Jesus says in the gospel of Matthew, "For I have come to call not the righteous but sinners," when he was asked about the people he liked to spend his time with.

Our wisdom traditions tell us that the root meaning of the word salvation is "the way of redemption" or "the way to wholeness." As we follow this line of thinking, we discover that our journey into wholeness, or "holiness" in the words of the mystical traditions, begins in a paradoxical way—not by

a search for peace and joy but by acknowledging
the grit and grist of life: suffering, illness, death, and
our alienation from ourselves and the depth of our
own spiritual and psychological capacities. In other
words, our journey begins with learning the meaning of compassion through our own experiences.
Now, this is a very important point: it is the full
acceptance of these aspects of ourselves that initi-
ates our journey into becoming fully human, fully
incarnated, and more open to joy.

Of course, we all want a good life. And when we
encounter life's difficulties, we want peace of mind
and good relationships, *and* we want to keep our
lifestyle and habits—the personalities we are used
to. And, of course, our culture supports this point
of view. The culture doesn't see our wounds and difficulties as calls for transformation. It sees them as
symptoms to alleviate so we can get back to "normal," which actually means functional in a social
way, not a spiritual, psychological, or even a personally fulfilling way.

Furthermore, most of us envision a life that is
successful, prosperous, and fulfilling, and if we have
children, we dream of a successful life for them. We
get angry with ourselves and with life when our
dreams and visions fail. But the failures of these
dreams and visions are very important, for they are
meant to awaken us to compassion—compassion
not only for others but for ourselves and for how

difficult life is.

Generally, we need our dreams of a good life to carry us into adulthood. But, later, we also need for these dreams to fail, in order to make way for our wholeness to begin to emerge and be discovered. And we need the self-compassion that these experiences can generate, in order to accept the difficulties in our lives as spiritual and psychological incubations and not as failures. Further, as we begin the work that Jung called "the realization of our shadow," we need this capacity for compassion in order to accept the poor, dispossessed, and disapproved part of ourselves.

To illustrate this point, I'll share with you the words of the Ba'al Shem Tov, founder of the Hassidic tradition in Judaism. He said, "There are many rooms in God's castle." Does that sound familiar? He then went on to say, "There is, however, one key that opens every room, and *that* key is a broken heart."

We need to have the courage and love to engage in life enough to have our hearts broken. Such broken hearts are not signs of failure. Rather, they open us to compassion and to becoming more fully human. These experiences not only humble us but also compel us to become aware of and outgrow our former selves and worldview.

Compassion, in its true sense, is the acceptance that life is full of difficulties and suffering. Accepting this reality and our ability to be in it, suffering with and caring about each other, brings us to the highest spiritual potentials in all of the great religions. Along with courage and love, compassion is a key to the fulfilling life for a person and for a culture. Again, I want to share with you seven principles I have used in my life, teaching, and writings to help cultivate compassion within ourselves one day at a time.

1. Compassion is difficult, because the way we usually think of it is as an ideal, seen from a distance. We prefer to assume we are compassionate even though we have not accepted our own suffering, responding to it instead with a fight or flight reaction. It might be helpful for you to review your thoughts about compassion. Why do you think we should become compassionate? Do you think making this journey to crack our hearts open is worthwhile?

2. Acceptance of suffering reminds us that self-compassion is needed, not self-judgement. Remember that acceptance is the necessary first step in transforming anything psychological. Our suffering may be caused by events, people, illnesses, inner conflicts, or the early or even later traumas in our life. But the healing path and our capacity to grow through and beyond our circumstances—that is, to transform our suffering—begins with self-compassion. Our compassion for ourselves is a cornerstone for having compassion for others.

3. We must value the inhabitants of our shadow, the parts of ourselves that we have disowned, devalued, rejected, and repressed. The great poet Rilke reminds us that "perhaps all the dragons of our lives are princesses who are only waiting to see us once beautiful and brave. Perhaps everything terrible is, in its deepest being, something that needs our love." This valuing means getting to know and understand—remember this doesn't mean embracing—some of our most negative feelings and self-critical voices. Journaling is very helpful not only for engaging in this step but for developing all of these principles. Keep in mind, nothing in our shadows scares us more, or needs our self-compassion more, than our own denied and impoverished potentials.

4. Compassion is in our nature. We are born helpless but ready to love and be loved. This reality means compassion is a basic part of our nature. We need to be cared for and we need to care for others. Unfortunately, in this time, we have developed a power-driven, achievement-oriented culture that wants us to adopt its values of success, rather than living by the values of the human heart. One of these is compassion for ourselves and others, as our great religions teach us. If we have stopped to think about it for a minute, we might wonder how we can be shocked at the rage, conflict, and alienation that has been erupting in our society over a long time.

5. Compassion calls for action. By *action*, I mean becoming sensitive to the needs of our own hearts and those of others. It is helpful to define what we think are compassionate actions toward ourselves and others. I've named some for you to consider in these principles. Once you have a list for yourself, see if you can convert it into a list of practices to follow day by day. Repeated practices lead us to cultivate a new awareness as our hearts are born anew into how we are living.

6. Compassion creates openness. To be compassionate to ourselves means being open to our shadow. We may be shocked and surprised to find more pain dwelling there than we imagined. The same is true when looking into our societal shadow. Developing compassion is a lifelong process because the more we develop the light of awareness, the more darkness is revealed. While this process may be startling at times, it should not be discouraging. As we do this work, more human potentials in ourselves and in our society will come into our conscious awareness. Take responsibility for understanding this process and for facing it in a curious, compassionate way.

7. Have compassion for your enemies, within and without. In her book *Twelve Steps to a Compassionate Life*, Karen Armstrong's final step is "Love Your Enemies." She isn't naive or sentimental about this step. She advises us to "look carefully and deeply into our own hearts and thus learn to see the sorrow of our enemy." She is talking about an enemy with a capital E, something or someone that seems to threaten our survival and everything we stand for— as the apocalypse is doing. We must keep in mind that compassion is a heart response. It seeks to suffer together and also to understand.

Neither of these actions means to acquiesce to or embrace. The first act of compassion is to seek to understand. Failing to understand an enemy within or without of ourselves, personally and collectively, is the guarantee of mounting strife.

Outrageous compassion takes both love and courage. I hope that from this brief look into compassion you will find that you can cultivate it, no matter how discouraged you might feel at times. Frankl in his great book about surviving the Nazi concentration camps, *Man's Search for Meaning*, writes that prisoners with compassion could reach beyond themselves to help others experience a humanity that made them feel that life had meaning and was endurable. The more we cultivate courage, love, and compassion in our lives, the better able we are to choose our responses in any given circumstances, to choose our own way, and even to become strong defenders of the values of the heart, of life.

———— ✦ ————

Thoughts and Questions to Ponder

Compassion, as I have pointed out, is not a term too many of us have a personal relationship with. Armstrong points out that it is the goal of most of the great religions. Can you write a personal response to what I have written about Jung's starting point for revitalizing compassion in our personal lives, which is reprinted below?

> Jung gives us the starting point for revitalizing the strength of compassion within ourselves. In Collected Works (vol. 11, par. 520–521), he writes that accepting ourselves with compassion is the first journey we must make. This point of view puts a whole new slant on how we were taught about compassion in the past. It challenges us in a more personal and profound way. We must suffer with ourselves, seek out the beggar, the infirm, the enemy, the stranger, and the criminal within ourselves. We must not preach but reflect. We must seek out the parts of ourselves we condemn, rage against, hide from the world, and deny from our awareness. We must be able to "give them the alms of our own kindness," seek not to embrace them but to understand them with compassion. This course brings true humility to us, and as this journey continues, we learn more about how to

live with wisdom and the practice of inner compassion flows outward.

As you explore more about compassion and yourself, respond in your journal to these lines I wrote:
"We need to have the courage and love to engage
in life enough to have our hearts broken. Such
broken hearts are not signs of failure. Rather, they
open us to compassion and to becoming more fully
human. These experiences not only humble us but
also compel us to become aware of and outgrow
our former selves and worldview. Compassion, in its
true sense, is the acceptance that life is full of difficulties and suffering. Accepting this reality and our
ability to be in it, suffering with and caring about
each other, brings us to the highest spiritual potentials in all of the great religions."

Please take your time and explore the reality behind these statements. How have you been taught
to think and feel about your own suffering?

These seven principles for cultivating compassion
are not commonly included in the perspective on
life we are taught as we grow up. I invite you to journal about each one and the feelings, thoughts, and
personal experiences they bring up in you.

List some of your enemies within and without, including some of your perceived political and societal enemies. Can you begin to see the humanity, fear, sorrow, sources of anger, and other human characteristics in them?

Other Thoughts?

PART IV

---·◆·---

Accepting the Challenges of the Heart

"We must take sides. Neutrality helps the oppressor, never the victim. Silence encourages the tormentor, never the tormented. Sometimes we must interfere. When human lives are endangered, when human dignity is in jeopardy, national borders and sensitivities become irrelevant. Wherever men and women are persecuted because of their race, religion, or political views, that place must—at that moment— become the center of the universe . . . our lives no longer belong to us alone; they belong to all those who need us so desperately."

—Elie Wiesel

The apocalypse is real and, as I pointed out, has many layers. It is a dark revelation of what our future will become if we fail to recognize the sacredness of every person and of all life. The pandemic, with so many terrible deaths, exposes how passive we have become in regard to the sacredness of life. It also shows us the violence with which some of us can deny the imminent possibility of the death of ourselves, those we care about, and even our planet.

The apocalypse is also unveiling harsh realities that have long existed in our lives and our society. It shows, as Armstrong notes in her books, that we haven't seen clearly enough that we all live in one world. Jung and most Jungian scholars and analysts agree with this perspective. When our shortsighted approaches to living and our value structures exclude and dispossess parts of ourselves and parts of humanity, they will come back to haunt us in destructive forms. And the belief that we can isolate ourselves from this reality is an illusion.

An apocalypse means we cannot go back to how we were before. Our previous state, incidentally, was not safe and secure, because it was sustaining the festering problems that now confront us.

We are faced with challenges that have no easy answers. Even the effort to fully understand them requires a collective transformation, a change in the heart of our social character. Since the 1970s we have developed a pattern of seeking quick solutions and appearing successful. We apply Band-Aid fixes to crises by treating symptoms, rather than searching for the more profound causes of our difficulties. If we try to follow this old pattern, the appearance of success will become more important than transformation, than revitalizing courage, love, and compassion. If we succumb to the compulsion to pursue successful appearances, we lose our ability to truly get to know ourselves, the depth of other people, and the nature of the crisis we are in. The secret here is that if enough people transform their hearts, then our society can truly change for the better.

Price, in the example I shared with you, challenges us to face an apocalypse by creating a "whole new life." To accept his challenge, we must have the courage to live with fear, anxiety, loss, and an unknown future. Accepting this challenge means fully choosing life and choosing to live not only with courage but also with love and compassion, which will become strength and realism in a very profound way. We now face challenges both personally and collectively. Our main concern must be with creating a different understanding of who we can be personally and together. Through this understanding, we can cultivate the ability and the will to create a new beginning for this country.

The Jungian position is that if we can face and make the needed transformation within ourselves, we can lessen, more effectively deal with, and in some cases even solve the threatening external events we face. If a sufficient number of people can have these experiences of transformation—having a change of heart that brings the focus of life away from power and back to love—we may be spared the worst possibilities of what is now facing us. I love the way Baldwin, as he ends his book *The Fire Next Time*, refers to the part of the apocalypse that was his major concern:

> Everything now, we must assume, is in our hands; we have no right to assume otherwise. If we—and now I mean the relatively conscious whites and the relatively conscious blacks, who must, like lovers, insist on, or create, the consciousness of the others—do not falter in our duty now, we may be able, handful that we are, to end the racial nightmare, and achieve our country, and change the history of the world. If we do not now dare everything, the fulfillment of that prophecy, re-created from the Bible in song by a slave is upon us: God gave Noah the rainbow sign, No more water, the fire next time!

He is right. The whole bigger picture is now in our hands. If we love life, ourselves, and the ones who are supposed to be dear to us, we must answer Price's question: "Who can you be and how can you get there, double-time?"

———— ⋅❖⋅ ————

Thoughts and Questions to Ponder

Reading this book has been a short but intense journey for most readers. I invite you to sit back, let its contents simmer in your mind, and then write about what comes up in your thoughts and feelings. Consider discussing them with people you feel comfortable with.

You might also note questions that come up for you that I haven't covered or thought about.

———— ⋅❖⋅ ————

ACKNOWLEDGEMENTS

A special thanks to my wife Dr. Massimillla Harris who urged me to develop these ideas and express them. She has walked hand in hand with me through this process as we have done since we first met.

I owe an intellectual debt to Dr. Edward Edinger for his book, *Archetype of the Apocalypse*, which gave me a structure for my reflections. The writings of Dr. C. G. Jung, especially in C.W. Vol. 10, "The Spiritual Problem in Modern Man," "The Undiscovered Self," and in C.W. vol. 11, "Answer to Job," have been of particular importance to me in the development of this book and my life. James Baldwin's, *The Fire Next Time*, and Reynolds Price's *A Whole New Life* have been rich sources of personal inspiration to me, as well as springs of creativity that bring life to the works of my intellect.

Courtney Tiberio deserves special mention for midwifing this book into the world and announcing its arrival. Julie Beckman-Key, my editor, has been helpful and creative in a manner that made this process enlarging and a pleasure. Sandi Tomlin-Sutker, my typist, performed the miracle of turning my handwriting into readable form.

My children and grandchildren have inspired and actually compelled me to have a profound sense of concern for the future they will be living in.

A NOTE OF THANKS

Whether you received *Facing the Apocalypse* as a gift, borrowed it from a friend, or purchased it yourself, we're glad you read it. We think that Bud Harris is a refreshing, challenging, and inspiring voice and we hope you will share this book and his thoughts with your family and friends. If you would like to learn more about Bud Harris, PhD, and his work please visit budharris.com or facebook.com/BudHarrisPh.D/.

ABOUT THE AUTHOR

Bud Harris, PhD, is a Jungian analyst, writer, and lecturer, who has dedicated his life to help people grow through their challenges and life situations to become "the best versions of themselves."

Originally a corporate businessman, Bud then owned his own business. Though very successful, he began to search for a new version of himself and his life at age thirty-five. He had become dissatisfied with his accomplishments in business and was being challenged by serious illness in his family.

Bud returned to graduate school to study psychotherapy. He earned his PhD in psychology and practiced as a psychotherapist and psychologist for several years. Later, Bud moved to Zurich, Switzerland, where he trained for over five years and graduated from the C. G. Jung Institute to become a Jungian analyst.

Bud is the author of sixteen informing and inspiring books. He writes and teaches with his wife, Jungian analyst Massimilla Harris, PhD, and lectures widely. Bud and Massimilla are practicing Jungian analysts in Asheville, North Carolina. For more information about Bud's practice and work, visit www.budharris.com and www.facebook.com/BudHarrisPh.D/.

CPSIA information can be obtained
at www.ICGtesting.com
Printed in the USA
LVHW102247151022
730802LV00003B/74